Your

Lungs

How Your BODY Works

Your Lungs

Anita Ganeri

Gareth Stevens Publishing
A WORLD ALMANAC EDUCATION GROUP COMPANY

ACKNOWLEDGMENTS

With thanks to: Frankie Iszard, Oliver Hood, Jade Hardie, Ben Ifrah, Diandra Beckles, Arron Henry, Sophie Raven. Models from Truly Scrumptious Ltd.

Please visit our web site at: www.garethstevens.com
For a free color catalog describing Gareth Stevens Publishing's
list of high-quality books and multimedia programs, call
1-800-542-2595 (USA) or 1-800-387-3178 (Canada).
Gareth Stevens Publishing's fax: (414) 332-3567.

Library of Congress Cataloging-in-Publication Data available upon request from publisher.
Fax (414) 336-0157 for the attention of the Publishing Records Department.

ISBN 0-8368-3634-0

This North American edition first published in 2003 by
Gareth Stevens Publishing
A World Almanac Education Group Company
330 West Olive Street, Suite 100
Milwaukee, WI 53212 USA

Original edition © 2003 by Evans Brothers Limited. First published in 2003 by Evans Brothers Limited, 2A Portman Mansions, Chiltern Street, London W1M 1LE, United Kingdom. This U.S. edition published under license from Evans Brothers Limited. This U.S. edition © 2003 by Gareth Stevens, Inc. Additional end matter © 2003 by Gareth Stevens, Inc.

Designer: Mark Holt
Artwork: Julian Baker
Photography: Steve Shott
Consultant: Dr. M. Turner

Gareth Stevens Editor: Carol Ryback
Gareth Stevens Designer: Katherine A. Goedheer

Photo credits:
Science Photo Library: CNRI, page 13; Professor P. Motta/Department of Anatomy/University "La Sapienza," Rome, page 15; NASA, page 18; Professors Motta, Correr, and Nottola/University "La Sapienza," Rome, page 21; David M. Martin, M.D., page 24.

Printed in the United States of America

1 2 3 4 5 6 7 8 9 07 06 05 04 03

Contents

How Do You Breathe?

You must breathe air to stay alive. As you breathe in, you pull fresh air into your body. Fresh air contains an important gas called **oxygen**. When you breathe, oxygen travels all around your body. Your body uses oxygen to keep you alive.

Your nose, mouth, **windpipe**, **lungs**, and **ribs** are the parts of your body that help you breathe. Together, they make up your **respiratory system**.

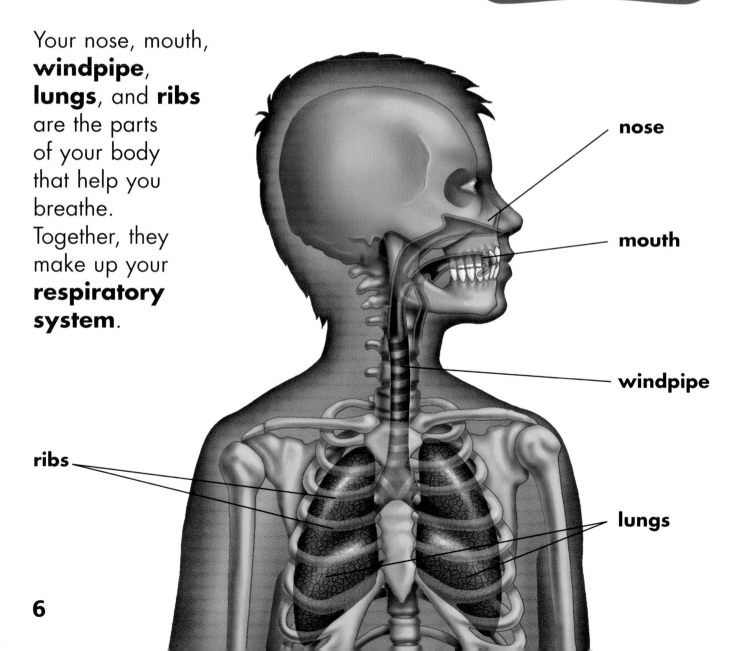

nose

mouth

windpipe

ribs

lungs

6

You probably don't think about breathing. It happens automatically. Your amazing brain controls your breathing. You breathe all the time, but you usually don't think about it.

How many candles can you blow out in one breath?

Good Air In

Take a deep breath. When you breathe in, air flows through your mouth or nose. The air travels down a large tube in your throat, called your windpipe. Inside your **chest**, your windpipe splits into two smaller tubes that lead into your two lungs. These two lung tubes keep splitting into even smaller tubes inside both of your lungs.

Amazing!
Your windpipe reaches down into your chest. It is about 4 inches (10 centimeters) long.

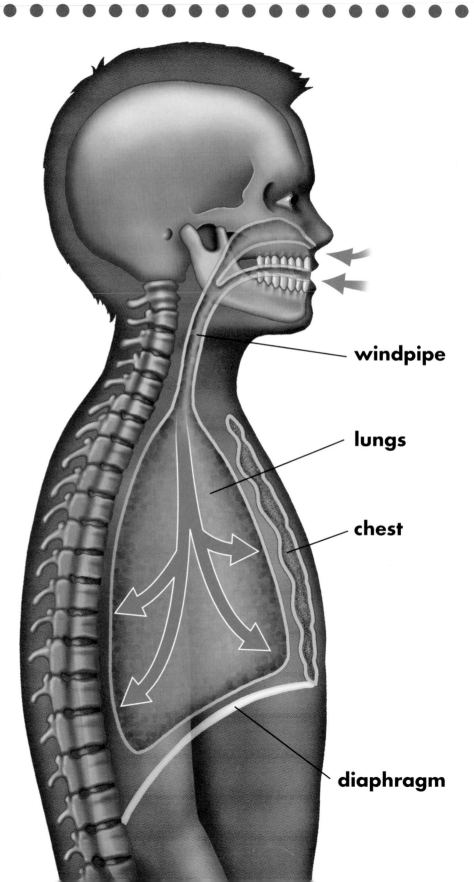

windpipe

lungs

chest

diaphragm

As you breathe in, your chest gets bigger so that your lungs have room to fill up with air. To make room, your ribs move up and out and a special flat muscle under your lungs moves downward. This muscle is called your **diaphragm**.

Do you ever **hiccup**? Hiccups happen when your diaphragm muscle twitches sharply as you breathe in. A sudden breath, or gasp, of air makes the "Hic" sound. As too much air rushes in, a flap at the top of your windpipe snaps shut. This makes the "Cup" sound. HICCUP!

Fold your arms across your chest and take a deep breath. Can you feel your chest get bigger?

9

Bad Air Out

As you breathe out, your ribs move down and your diaphragm muscle moves up. This action squeezes stale air out of your two lungs. Stale air moves out from your lungs into your windpipe. You blow the stale air out of your windpipe through your nose or mouth.

You use air flowing out of your lungs to whistle. Not everyone can whistle. Can you?

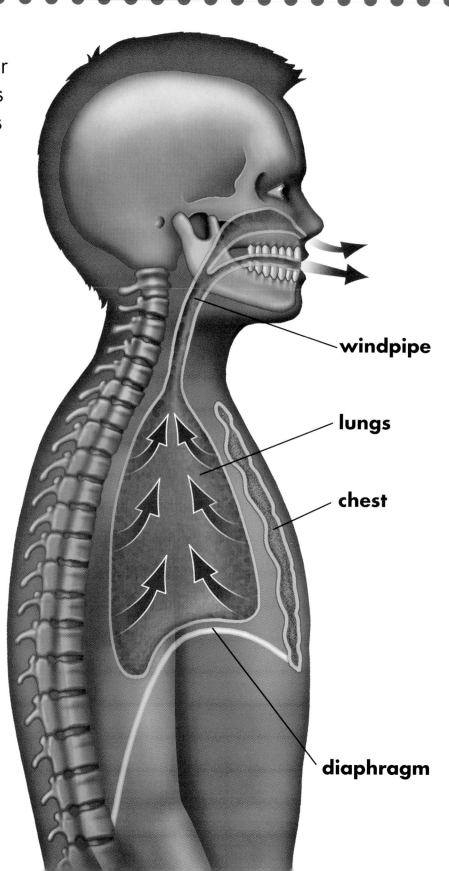

windpipe

lungs

chest

diaphragm

10

The stale air you push out of your lungs contains a gas called **carbon dioxide**. You must breathe out stale air that carries carbon dioxide, or it can harm your body.

You usually cannot see the air you breathe out unless it's a cold day. Cold weather makes your breath look like puffs of steam. The puffs are made of tiny drops of water in your breath.

Amazing!

When you blow up a party balloon, you are filling it with old, stale air.

Your Lungs

Your lungs are like two spongy bags inside your chest. Your two lungs are not the same size. Your left lung is slightly smaller than your right lung to make enough room in your chest for your heart.

Tiny air tubes lead from your windpipe into your lungs. The air tubes end in tiny air sacs called **alveoli** (el-VEE-o-lie). When you breathe in, your alveoli fill up with air.

The tiny alveoli in your lungs lie next to each other like grapes in a bunch.

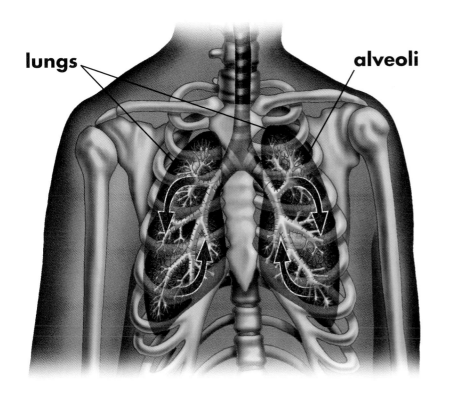

lungs　**alveoli**

Amazing!

If you could spread the alveoli in your lungs out flat, they would cover one side of a singles tennis court!

Oxygen from the air enters your lungs and seeps through the alveoli into your blood. Your blood carries the oxygen around your body. Your blood also carries carbon dioxide from your body to your alveoli, so you can breathe the carbon dioxide out of your lungs. You have about 600 million alveoli in your lungs. Each of these tiny air sacs is about the size of a pinpoint, but together they form a very large area inside your lungs.

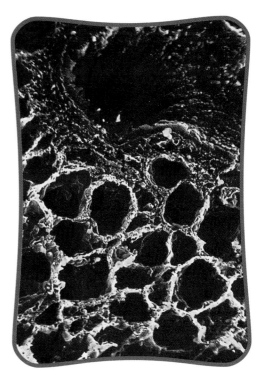

Under a microscope, your alveoli look like tiny air sacs.

Red Blood

Your blood travels through your body in tiny tubes called **blood vessels**. The blood vessels in your lungs are right next to your alveoli. Your **red blood cells** pick up oxygen from your alveoli and carry it around your body. The oxygen in your red blood cells gives blood its bright red color.

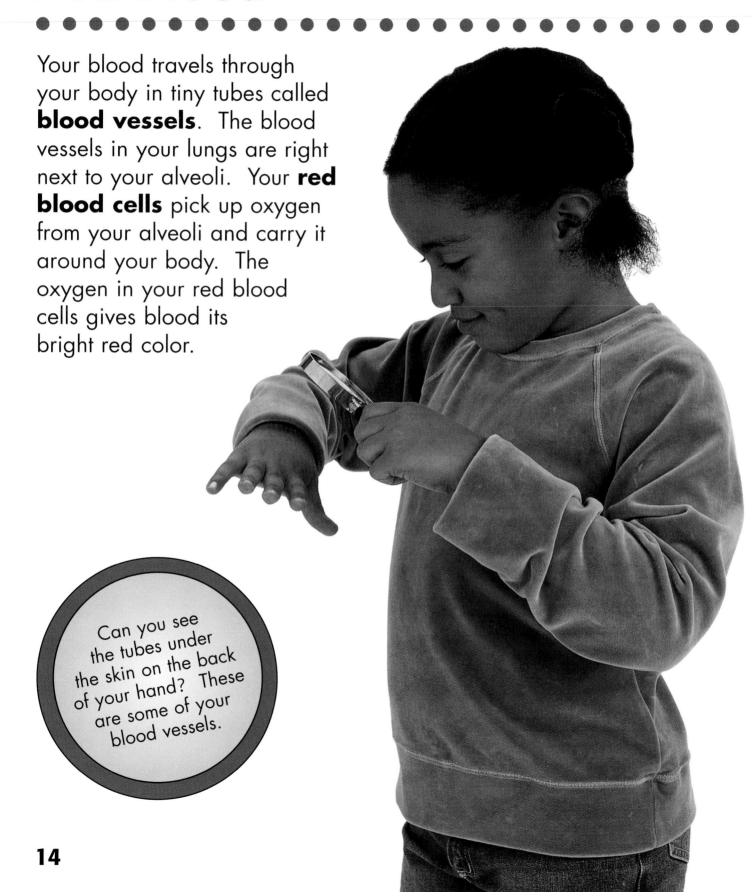

Can you see the tubes under the skin on the back of your hand? These are some of your blood vessels.

The bright red blood traveling around your body changes color as it moves along. Your blood changes color because it is trading the oxygen it carries for the carbon dioxide waste gas made by your body. As your blood takes on more carbon dioxide, it turns dark red. Your dark red blood travels back to your lungs. Your lungs breathe out the carbon dioxide.

Amazing!

Your body has about 30 million red blood cells that carry oxygen. New red blood cells are made deep inside the **bone marrow** in your bones.

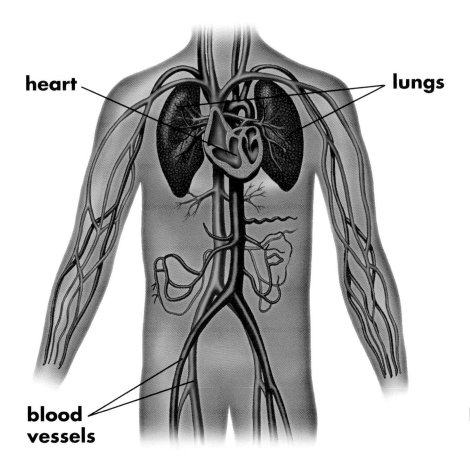

heart

lungs

blood vessels

New red blood cells are made inside your bone marrow.

Enough Air?

You need to breathe all the time, or your body would die. Your amazing brain keeps your lungs breathing. If you hold your breath too long, your brain makes you breathe again.

The number of times you breathe in and out depends on your age. Someone your age probably breathes about thirty times in just one minute. Most adults will breathe about fifteen times in one minute.

Amazing!

In one day, you breathe enough air to fill about 500 party balloons.

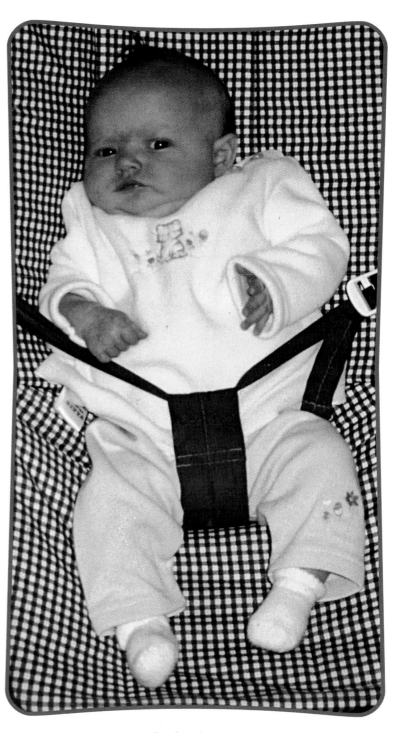

A young baby breathes about forty times in a minute.

The amount of air you need for each breath depends on what you are doing. In a normal breath, you take in about one cupful of air. When you run, you take in about ten times that much. Your moving body breathes faster because it needs a lot of oxygen for **energy**. When you are asleep, your body hardly moves and needs less oxygen. You breathe in less air when you sleep than when you run.

You feel tired after running because your body needs to replace all the oxygen you have just used up.

High Up and Deep Down

Some places have very little air or no air at all. The higher up a mountain you climb, the less oxygen there is in the air for you to breathe. Air with little oxygen in it is sometimes called "thin air." Mountain climbers often carry tanks of extra oxygen to breathe while they are climbing high up in the mountains.

People who live in the mountains all year long do not have trouble breathing the thin air. Their blood can carry more oxygen because their blood makes extra red blood cells. The extra red blood cells help them breathe more easily on the mountaintop.

Amazing!

Hardy mountain animals, such as llamas, carry more oxygen in their blood, just like people who live high in the mountains.

An astronaut on the Moon must carry air to breathe.

There is no air in outer space. The astronauts who landed on the Moon carried special air tanks on their backs. The tanks let them breathe air through their helmets.

There is no air to breathe underwater, so **scuba divers** carry their own air supply. They carry tanks of air on their backs and can breathe the air through a special mouthpiece. As a scuba diver breathes out, bubbles of stale air rise in the water.

A snorkel tube reaches to the surface of the water so you can breathe air while swimming underwater.

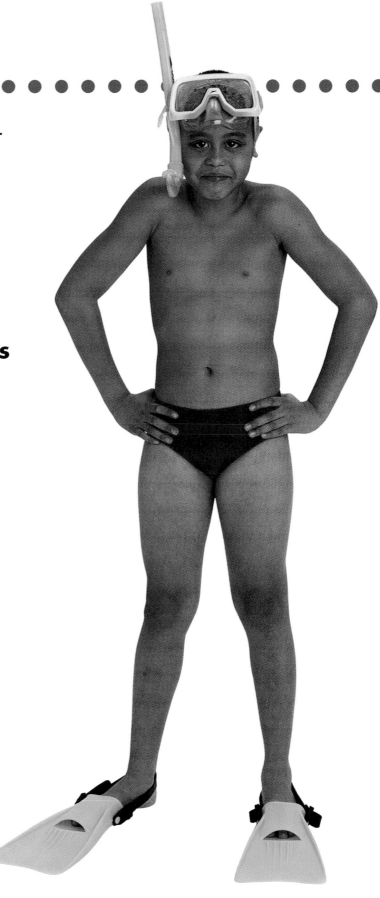

Healthy Lungs

When you are born, your lungs are pale pink, but they turn darker as you get older. Dust, dirt, and **germs** in the air you breathe make your lungs dirty. Your body works to keep your lungs as clean as possible. The inside of your nose is lined with tiny hairs and a slimy **mucus**. Dirt and germs stick to mucus as you breathe. You help your body get rid of dirt and germs when you blow your nose.

Your body makes extra mucus when you have a cold. Extra mucus catches the cold germs so you can blow them out of your body.

Your air tubes are also lined with mucus and covered with tiny hairs called **cilia**. The mucus and cilia in your air tubes catch dirt and germs and push them away from your lungs.

When people smoke cigarettes, they breathe in harmful **chemicals**. These chemicals stop the cilia from working, so dirt and mucus clog up the lungs. Smoking can cause serious illnesses, such as **cancer** and **heart disease**.

Amazing!

Fumes from cars, trucks, factories, and power plants add dust and dirt to the air.

A microscope can show the cilia in your air tubes that work to catch dirt and germs.

Sneezes and Coughs

Aaatchooo! What makes you sneeze? Dust and germs can get in your nose. You sneeze to get rid of them. When you sneeze, you take a sudden breath that shuts off your nose and throat. The air builds up in your lungs and blasts out through your nose and mouth. Sneezing clears dust and germs from your nose. A sneeze can travel at over 100 miles (160 kilometers) per hour.

Amazing!

Flower **pollen** floating in the air makes some people sneeze. They have an **allergy** to the flower pollen.

Like sneezing, coughing helps clear out your air tubes. Sneezing and coughing can also spread germs. When you have a cold, the air you sneeze or cough out contains millions of cold germs. If other people breathe in your germs, they may catch your cold. You cannot always stop a sneeze or a cough, but you should always sneeze or cough into a tissue to keep from spreading germs.

A bad cough can make your throat hurt. An adult might give you some syrupy cough medicine to make your throat feel better.

Speaking and Singing

You use your air tubes for speaking and singing, too. Look in a mirror and swallow. That lump on the outside of your throat is your **voicebox**. Inside your throat, two thin strings of muscle called your **vocal folds** lie across your voicebox. When you speak, air flows over them and makes them **vibrate**. The vibrating produces the sound of your voice. Your lips, teeth, tongue, nose, and throat shape those sounds into words. Your voice makes sounds from a quiet whisper to a very loud scream.

Amazing!

The enormous blue whale has the loudest voice of any creature. Its voice can travel about 160 miles (257 km).

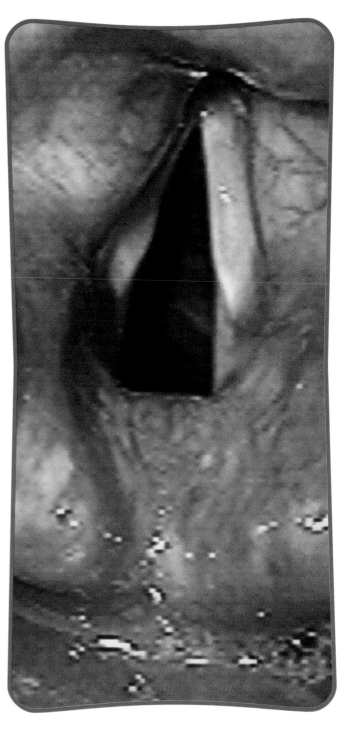

The vocal folds in your throat vibrate when you talk or sing.

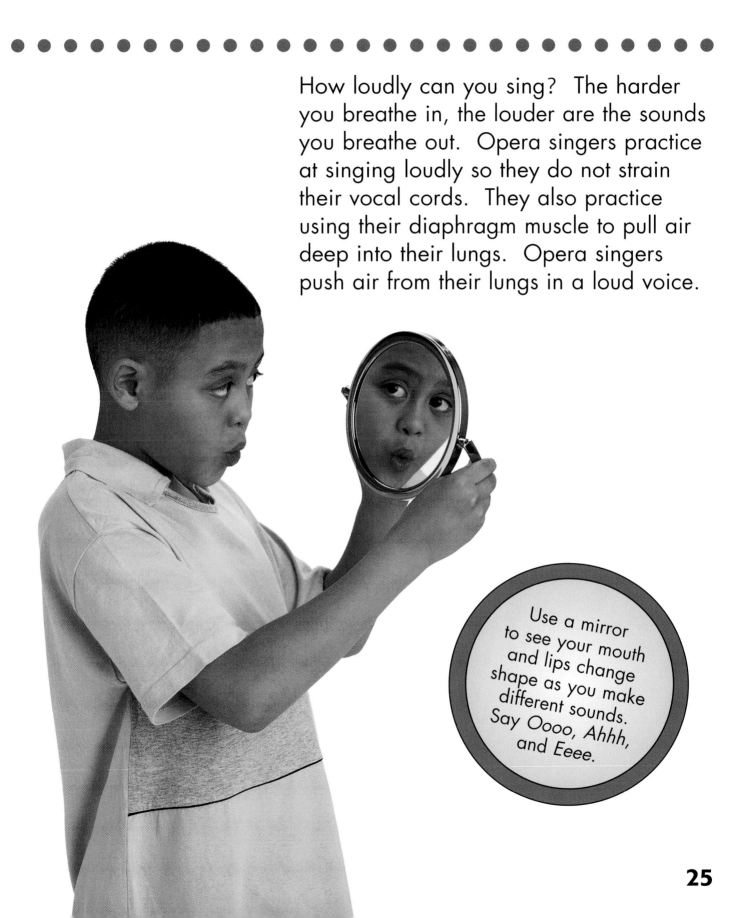

How loudly can you sing? The harder you breathe in, the louder are the sounds you breathe out. Opera singers practice at singing loudly so they do not strain their vocal cords. They also practice using their diaphragm muscle to pull air deep into their lungs. Opera singers push air from their lungs in a loud voice.

Use a mirror to see your mouth and lips change shape as you make different sounds. Say Oooo, Ahhh, and Eeee.

Activity

Your respiratory system has different parts. How many parts can you name? Photocopy page 27 and match the numbers below to the body parts listed on page 27.

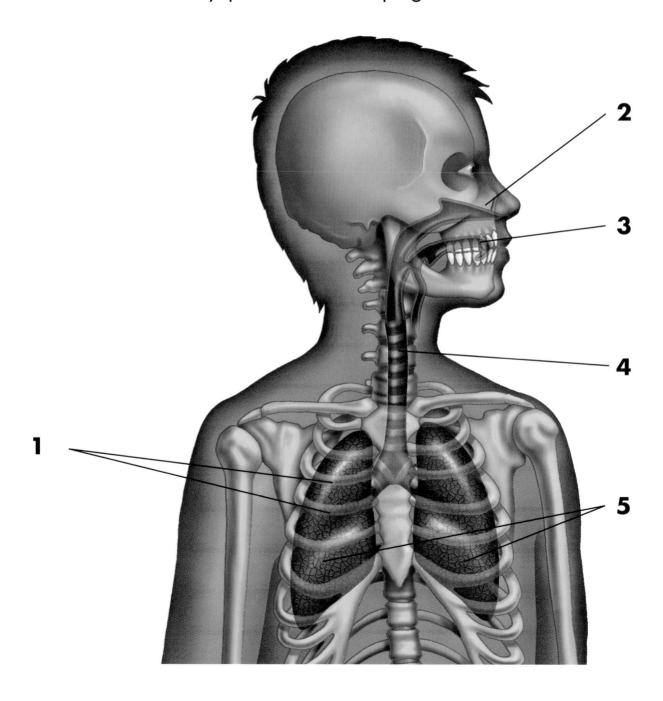

_____ **nose**

_____ **ribs**

_____ **lungs**

_____ **mouth**

_____ **windpipe**

Glossary

allergy: a strong reaction, such as sneezing or coughing, to a substance that might not make others sneeze or cough.

alveoli: tiny air sacs found deep in your lungs. Alveoli have very thin walls that let oxygen from the air you breathe pass into your blood. They also let carbon dioxide pass out of your blood and into your lungs to breathe out.

blood vessels: tiny, flexible tubes that carry blood around your body.

bone marrow: the jellylike material inside your bones that makes new blood cells.

cancer: a disease that makes body cells grow out of control.

carbon dioxide: a waste gas carried by your blood that you need to breathe out.

chemicals: substances that take part in a process causing something to change.

chest: the upper part of your body that contains your lungs.

cilia: tiny hairs that line your air tubes and trap dust and germs that enter your body.

diaphragm: a flat sheet of muscle under your lungs that moves down as you breathe in and up as you breathe out.

energy: the power that lets something move or do work.

fumes: smoke that contains pieces of dust and dirt.

germs: tiny living things that cause some illnesses.

heart disease: an illness that makes the heart muscle or its blood vessels not work right.

hiccup: a funny sound caused by a sudden twitching of your diaphragm muscle and the snapping shut of a tiny flap at the top of your windpipe as you breathe in air quickly.

lungs: two spongy bags inside your chest that hold air.

mucus: the slimy stuff that lines your nose, air tubes, and lungs and helps protect them from germs and dirt.

oxygen: a gas in the air that you must breathe to live.

pollen: a very fine dust made by flowers and weeds.

red blood cells: special cells in your blood that carry oxygen around your body.

respiratory system: the parts of your body that work together to help you breathe.

ribs: curved bones in your chest that protect your lungs.

scuba divers: underwater swimmers who carry an air supply in a tank on their backs and breathe the air in the tank through a special tube and mouthpiece. Scuba is short for **s**elf-**c**ontained **u**nderwater **b**reathing **a**pparatus.

vibrate: to move quickly back and forth or side to side.

vocal folds: thin muscles that lie across your voicebox and vibrate to produce sounds.

voicebox: an area in your throat with muscles that help you speak. You see it from outside your body as a lump under the skin on your throat.

windpipe: the main tube leading down your throat and into your lungs.

More Books to Read

Body Cycles. Cycles (series).
   Michael Elsohn Ross
   (Millbrook Press)

Breathing. Body Books (series).
   Anna Sandeman
   (Copper Beech Books)

Breathing Well. Body Works
   (series). Paul Bennett
   (Silver Press)

The Respiratory System.
   Human Body Systems (series).
   Helen Frost (Pebble Books)

Why Can't I Breathe
   Underwater? Body Wise
   (series). Sharon Cromwell
   (Heinemann Library)

Why Do I Sneeze? Body
   Matters (series). Angela
   Royston (Heinemann Library)

Videos

Human Body for Children.
   (series) (Schlessinger Video)

Just the Facts: The Human Body.
   (Goldhil Home Media)

Web Sites

BrainPOP: Respiratory System.
   www.brainpop.com/health/
   respiratory/

Why Do We Breathe?
   www.sk.lung.ca/content.cfm/
   kbreathe

Index